The Flowering of Flint
New and Selected Poems

PETER ABBS was born and grew up on the North Norfolk coast in England. He has written and lectured widely on the nature of creativity and the poetics of culture. In 2004 he was Writer-in-Residence at Lyon College, Arkansas. He is the Poetry Editor of *Resurgence* and editor of *Earth Songs*, the first Anglo-American anthology of contemporary eco-verse. He has published seven volumes of poetry including *Icons of Time*, *Personae* and *Viva la Vida*. He is currently Research Professor of Creative Writing at the University of Sussex.

Also by Peter Abbs

For Man and Islands (1978)
Songs of a New Taliesin (1981)
Icons of Time (1991)
Personae (1996)
Angelic Imagination (1997)
Love After Sappho (1999)
Viva la Vida (2005)

The Flowering of Flint:
New and Selected Poems

PETER ABBS

SALT

CAMBRIDGE

PUBLISHED BY SALT PUBLISHING
PO Box 937, Great Wilbraham, Cambridge PDO CB21 5JX United Kingdom

First published 2007

Printed and bound in the United Kingdom by Lightning Source

Typeset in Swift 9.5/13

ISBN 978 1 84471 313 4 paperback

Salt Publishing Ltd gratefully acknowledges
the financial assistance of Arts Council England

10 1 3 5 7 9 8 6 4 2

For D

Contents

Foreword

Poetry's primary task is to break, blow, burn and make us new. It is also, at other times, to perplex and unsettle, to keep us somewhat unstable and open to change. If some of the poems gathered here bring about either of these states, then I am more than satisfied.

These poems have been written over the last twenty eight years. They have been selected from seven previous volumes, the first being published in 1978, the last in 2005. I have discarded all poems that seemed to me to fail for whatever reason. I have kept revisions to a minimum, deciding (after some struggle) I had little choice but to accept the voice each poem was originally written in.

I have added or cut a few section headings but only to make the thematic concerns clearer or to enhance the flow of the poems. In all cases, the changes have been minimal.

Finally, I have added a number of new poems at the end. I hope these express further developments in my work, so that *The Flowering of Flint* is not only retrospective but, also, prospective—for I would like to think that I am not comfortably settling down, but keeping faith with the ineffable spirit of life itself.

Peter Abbs

Acknowledgements

Some of the poems in this volume have been previously published in: *Acumen, Agenda, Caduceus, Interpreter's House, London Magazine, Magma, International Poetry Review, Poetry Wales, Resurgence, Scintilla, Sea of Faith, South, Stand, Tears in the Fence, Temenos Review, The Poet's Voice* and *Urthona*.

The poem 'The Flowering of Flint' was commissioned by East Sussex County Council.

From
For Man and Islands
1978

Prelude

Where would you lead
   me and what
      would you have of
me, restless
   and enigmatic
      spirit? In
the enclosed garden
   it is again
      Autumn. Sycamore
leaves litter the
   small paths—
      the jagged leaves'
edges are turned
   inwards and everywhere
      their yellowness is
marred and blotched
   with blight. In
      the garden
the lemon light grows
   faint. Yet what
      are *you* doing
here, lover of
   strange mists and burning
      aromas,
at the open
   gate standing with
      the palms of your
hands showing? Will
   you wait as
      I approach and
let me read and
   go where the lines
      take me?

The Word

You suggest and
provoke until
I chase,

chase you wherever
you will,
I would, but

where do you
go,
down which

turning, into
which
unused chapel of truth,

so many the turnings,
crosses,
ends, I do not know—

yet, tantalizer, how
can I
forget how

you beckon so, what
you would
promise

in your lithe movement,
not to be mine,
grace

in my city,
out
of my power.

[4]

It

It skulks in the mind's undergrowth
in the dark thickets
it quivers close to the bed of rivers
a snake through the conflagration of grass
it is acquainted with stones and roots
has wound itself many times round
the dripping tentacles of nature

at dusk it flies through the warp and weft of shadows
compounds the darkness
till large familiar things loom forward
bulked with strangeness
blackness humped upon blackness
through which it lilts and slips

where do I stand but where it was
and is no longer though
something of its essence always lingers
hangs frailly in the morning
from the bent bough's sodden foliage
pervades a corner of the garden
a turning of the road

disquieted I poke the ground
dank arching grass blank stones
a thistlehead unloads its seeds
a bird flits through the charcoal thickets
the silence drums
I tread near the edge of some archaic memory
I can never reach
and spill a brief life writing
to allay the ache of it

The Death of Three Cocks

He came punctually, at eleven, the hour he said.
I took him to the shed.
He upturned the first bird
And slipped the knife into its neck.

More crimson than its crown,
The blood dripped to the ground—
Shocking in its redness—
And with one hand he kept the rent

Neck down. Mildly, he said
I have seen this since I was a child
Following the heels of the butcher
Round the farms.

With a kind of inward dread I took
The dead bird from his hands.
There was such commotion in its legs
And pinions, it appalled to hold it.

Obedient to the last transmission
Of the will, its mottled wings
Still fluttered, shut and shuddered—
Would not stay still.

Yet I must stand and watch
The next two go, wedged upside down between
The farmer's legs, to know
That somewhere in that ruffled sheen

My neighbour's knife had broken through
And watch the bird's panic and premonition ebb
As, across their bright bead eyes,
Slowly the coarse lids drooped and set.

Furtively, I shovelled soil upon the blood.
The children must not know nor guess.
It is the last time! Once is enough! I said.
For hours I gathered up the incriminating fluff.

At the farm that afternoon another batch of cocks were bled.

Evening after the Maelstrom

For the Darlington Family

It is evening, after the maelstrom,
After the upturning,
Burning and devastation of cities,
As reported on radio—
And (briefly) on television.
And prophesied in the last newspapers.

The herd stand by the farm's gate,
Dumb and enduring.
Even in this breeze, bitter
With mountain mist and drizzle,
Their ribbed flanks are calm as boulders—
Only their frayed tails twitching.

They have stood there
Ten thousand years, bulging
Eyes staring down
The dark track, trailing back
Through the charred centuries,
To the first spark of history.

Slathering, their warm breath
Wreathes the air; they await
Man's archaic canticle to cattle,
And a half-simple girl who wades
Slowly through the slang's
Slop and mud to guide them in.

The door opens on to dusty hay,
Bedding for a dozen animals.
Through the dark slates' cracks light
Needles the barbarian night—
Inside, at the finger's touch,
Thick milk drums into the pails.

From
Songs of a New Taliesin
1981

Good Friday

And on the Friday
Mary Magdalene
came to her Christ,

hung on the cross,
a noble bird,
stripped of his plumage,

his white skin
ripped, his quivering wings
pinned to the wood,

and she lay with him
and in his great pain
he made manifest his love.

And on the next day
the bloody tree
burst into bud,

and migrating flocks perched
on the outstretched arms.
And there was song.

This Nomadic God

1

When the God was born on the hill we stayed inside.

2

When we spotted in the valley his bloody caul making the
    stream all red,
Somewhat repelled, we walked away.

3

When on the same night we stared into his great eye
Glaring through our window we switched off the light;
We said: *There can be no such thing.*
Not in our times, 2000 Anno Domini.

4

When in the darkness he dared to rise through the basement of
    our house
We fumbled for the light and cried: *Ah! Dreams!—and their archaic*
remnants.
For we had read the literature. And sighed, relieved.

5

Later, when the trees' leaves shrivelled yellow,
Later, when the bent bracken bled profusely,
Later, when the low snow clouds shed their icy shingle,
Later, when the white river no longer flowed but lay nailed to its
    own bed—
If you remember—and to be fair—we were both rather busy;
There were forms to sign, bills to clear,
And the house—it stood in constant need of attention and repair.

6

Yet still the conjuror-god casts his signs about,
Daily scrawls his icons on the shifting sands;
Above reeling cities brushes his gentle ideograms,
On concrete slabs executes his reckless graffiti.

7

And still, on random days, he knocks on our locked door
Many times. Incisive knocks. Insistent. What would he have of
    us?
This trickster salesman, this nomadic god? If we let him in,
Would he annihilate our private space?
At our table does he want a simple place?
Is it that he wants a glass of wine? A slice of bread?
Two stale lives to transubstantiate?

From
Icons of Time
1991

Prologue

Who I Am

He did not observe that with all his efforts he made no advance—
meeting no resistance that might, as it were, serve as a support upon
which he could take a stand, to which he could apply his powers,
and so set his understanding in motion.

Kant

What is it that I do? This dizzy spinning
Of myself. This geometric cobweb that I make
From my own entrails. Intractable substance,
Obsessively shaped to a fine thread.
Part fact. Part fabulation. An obscure agent
In me fashioning the dark strands into pattern,
A design, somehow redemptive, however difficult.
What was could not have been otherwise.
There's a kind of freedom in admitting it.
Facts are weights. They tether random flight,
The delusions of Icarus, the Romantic type.
Filament by filament, inch by inch, I make
This architecture: a bound and limited life.
What I have struggled with is who I am.

Fragments from a Catholic Childhood

I rhyme to see myself, to set the darkness echoing.

—SEAMUS HEANEY

Premature Birth

Surname: Abbs. *First names*: Peter Francis.
Date of birth: 22.2.42. *Place*: Cromer.
The facts console, deceive and mesmerize.
Yet mother's story has a nightmare ring.
All the way to the theatre she had screamed:
I want to die, I want to die, I want—
Until the gas took over. Born premature—
Cut from the womb three months too soon—
I choked into the commotion of hands, the glare
Of swivelling lights, muffled blare of plenitude.
Mother sighed *A girl? A girl?* and bitter, wept.
For her: scars from the surgeon's knife.
For me: slow, impeded waking into life.

At the Oak Woods

This morning, not as it usually is.
Not box-hedge, nor black currant, nor mint's aroma.
Merely the breeze tapping the window pane—
And Grandmother's there. With pins, with clips, she plaits
Her hair. Grandfather's sipping tea from his saucer.
I've slipped the intervening years again.
On the fire branches froth, sizzle, blaze, smoulder.
The varnished chairs shimmer like manufactured glass,
Their curving legs are tongues of fire.
I go down the green passage to the open door,
Splinters of God lie in the melting grass.
The marigolds stand erect, orange and oracular.
I go through the walled garden to the pond.
A goldfish surfaces. Circles. And is gone.

Unread Signs

Earth was littered with signs we did not read
Nor comprehend. In gaping pits we picked
Glossy blackberries or collected from the ground
Cold metal shapes, long, tapered, with frilled edges—
Chock-full with grit and sand. Harder than shale
Whatever force had forged them, they were made to last.
Blankly we accepted them, bits from dislodged turf,
Fragments of the sliding screes we tried to scale.
Barbed wire poked through bramble thickets
Or dangled, flaking, from the cliff's ledges.
We dived into a labyrinth of tunnels
Rank with urine and discarded papers.

Shells exploded, ships sank, burning cities fell.
We hurtled through the black, blind, ephemeral.

The Look-out Tower in the Oak Woods

We saw only what our guileless games allowed;
Assumed the shelter's womb led out towards
The light. Always summer. The sea a sheet
Of wrinkled blue (on blue) with puffs of cloud;
No shadows ran along the silent beach—
Norfolk's backdrop to our blindfold play.
In the Oak Woods we climbed the look-out tower.
We leapt the missing steps. From the broken top
We watched the yellow squares streaked with scarlet
End abruptly with the shore. Low tide.
Stranded on the white chalk bed, a mine
Stared back at us with one blank eye;

But we stood up high, salt on our lips and brow,
Safe on the rotting planks—the moment, always now.

Myrtle Cottage at West Runton

The West Runton Abbs were Methodists.
They ate meat on Fridays, placed no crucifixes
On the mantelpiece, read *Pilgrim's*
Progress and *The Methodist Recorder*. *Papists!*
Grandmother spits out the word like it burns
Her mouth. Grandfather keeps himself apart.
Where the coast road turns to Roman Camp
He sits on the village bench and talks Socialism.
I don't believe in any God you dress
Up for, he says. *And read between the lines!*
All his life he laboured for the genteel classes
He most despised. In Myrtle Cottage
A wood fire glows. Dark above the old bureau
An antlered stag stands high,
                                        where water flows.

The Other Child

I look through the window of my first school:
St Joseph's. R. C. Sheringham. Norfolk.
Through the pane of fractured glass I stare
Into that silent chamber, sunk from mind.
Silver radiators still stand by the dark green
But all the trappings—abacus, globe,
Charts, blackboard, maps—have long since gone.
Was I ever here? Learning God by rote?
Obscure eel in the shallow tank of learning—
Even then forgetful of names, dates, facts.
I cannot find the child I was. Nothing
Coheres. Or coincides. Or rhymes.

The school door's locked; the place is out of bounds.
A pensive boy inside does not turn round.

Waiting for the Harvester

Here I stood in the crew-cut stubble,
Sharp stone in hand waiting for the harvester
To turn upon the final strip of wheat,
To see the hares dart wide-eyed into the gun's
Explosion or rise like crimson rags upon
The blades. Now, near the same spot I can
Hardly recognize the self I was;
Now I am no longer armed—I move
Across the earth, mesmerized; myself
Trapped in the last small track of wilderness.
At every footfall, at every dog bark,
Every quiver of the vast machine, I shudder.
Sense in my flesh my own sharp stone;
The damp blades whirring above dry bone.

The Loss of Faith

What did we do when we unchained the earth from its sun?
. . . Are we not plunging continually?
. . . Are we not straying as through an infinite nothing?

—Nietzsche

Who put the neon-lighting of his childhood
Out? A juke box throbs with *Jail House Rock.*
He reads Karl Marx and dreams of freedom;
He smoothes his hair with daubs of Brylcream.
Gone from the Eucharist, where is God?
On Sheringham sands *I can connect nothing*
With nothing. The spray lashes into the dark.
In my own town I have become a stranger.
I kneel and pray before the blessed virgin—
My mind's a stew where Magdalene strips.
I enquire of all that lives its final aim.
The ornate dome of faith cracks and splits.

God created the world *ex nihilo.* And withdrew.
Then, one day, the nothingness seeped through.

Father and Son

Spirit gains its truth only by finding itself in absolute dismemberment.

—HEGEL

Tongue-Tied

Father, now when I speak, I speak for you.
The silence you maintained could not be kept.
A knife, it spliced our mutual lives in two.
Tongue-tied, we were forever awkward. And inept.
Silence was our dumb inheritance,
The suicidal note passed down to us:
Keep your tongue still. Keep your mouth shut—
Numbing contract of our rural class.
The laconic words were slowly drawled
To dam our thoughts and let the feelings pass.
Nothing. Say nothing. Say nothing at all.
The anger mounting in the throat was swallowed back;
And swallowed back it became all hell to know
What the dumb thing was, which choked us so.

Language!

Father, what was it which divided us?
It crawled without a name. It grew in our
Embarrassment. A freak. An albatross
Worn privately. Yet it came from a power
Outside. *The 44 Education Act. The New Welfare.*
This weekly drama comes drifting back.

My brother has returned from Paston School.
He does his language homework in the parlour;
Declines regular nouns, corrects bad grammar.
Father, you scan *The Mirror* on the kitchen stool:
Jesus Christ! The bitch went down! Bloody Hell!
Fucked up m'bleedin Vernon's Pools as well!

Language! Language! Language! I hear my mother gasp.
The curtains hang like iron across the glass.

Generations of Farm Hands

A metal sky weighs upon the horizontal land,
Drained, dyked, undemonstrative.
After all these years, I work to understand:
Give the silence a voice, the resentment tongue,
To brand it indelible on the fugitive mind.
Where did it begin, that subterranean anger,
Smouldering, barely exploding, quickly subsiding?
Chill ash. The lava of embarrassment.
Was it being born rural working-class?
Generations of farmhands, time out of mind,
Forcing their feelings down till they drowned
To resurrect, embittered, against their own kind.

Civilization's dismemberment of man. Not hearts.
Not heads. Not tongues. But hands, severed hands.

Predicament

Father, what was it made us quell our convictions?
Tame our moving tongues? We had no politics.
No public thoughts. Our feelings became convicts
Without right of expression. Tortured by shame
They couldn't announce themselves in the boisterous
Square nor exonerate their names.
We hadn't the heart to claim the beauty of anger;
The pride of justice. Whatever truth stirred
In our shallow lives, we hammered down.
Daily, we slew our aspiring selves and deemed
It wise. *Well, who the fuck does he think he is?*
Too clever by half!
Cut him down to size!
Yet, all the time, the bitter sea spoke otherwise.

Winter Visit

Day staggers in, glazed-eyed, an invalid.
Morning contracts to shrunken appetites.
Little endures that interests you much.
Something like tears slide down the glass.
Your allotment, hard won, reverts to wilderness.
The fertile square is now couch grass.
Downstairs the chiming clock conveys a measured
Sense of things, not our snapped thread
Where beads in darkness scatter out of reach
Under the silent bed, under the silent past.
Nothing culminates. I walk the beach—
The Bingo's boarded up, the glass pane's smashed.
I sidle the length of my childhood cage.
An empty bench observes the breaking waves.

A Conversation with the Doctor
at the Time of the Chernobyl Disaster

You stand at the window in your striped pyjamas,
Like a disaster victim, and I am outside.
It is the second of May. The hawthorn blossom
Froths and blows all over Sheringham.
The doctor takes me to his car and says:
Your father hasn't much longer to go.
Over our heads the arctic clouds explode
And mushroom. *He has the worst heart I know.*
The wind, unseen, plucks at our hair and clothes.
He is living on borrowed time. And pills.
I catch you at the window waiting for news.
There's nothing; nothing more medicine can do.

You turn to me, taciturn: *What did he say?*
And all about us spreads cancerous May.

Crisis

As a child destroys a toy it has become
Indifferent to, so nature has it in for you.
Once partisan, now it doesn't care a jot;
It knows precisely where, when, how you'll crack.
The plastic bottles untidy the tidy house.
You swallow pills for urine, pills for gout,
Pills for sleep and now tranquillisers to ease
The dying. For two days they knock you out.
You drift among us, neither living nor dead.
Then the waves of pain come surging back;
They break over your hallucinating head.
All night you drown for want of common breath.
Day washes up the mess. Nothing's to be done.
A holocaust sky blots out the sun.

November Garden

This November's slow. An aging sun weeps cold
On stone. You remain an invalid in bed.
Your body's shrunk. You lie small as a child.
I won't fucking mend this time, you said.
Your mind meanders through a maze its own.
The clinical air blasts my face and head.
And all you want is to be left alone.

This garden's become a place I almost dread.
A rectangle of smoking foliage. More gaps
Than substance. What fruit remains is cut and hollow.
The weight of barren years drags down my steps.
I recall early frosts, the drifting snow,
Snow that, once, as we walked, filled in our tracks—
Snow that was always driving in, behind our backs.

Other Memories

Father, I've been unjust to you.
Less than fair. Large with my own self.
Janus, the two-faced god, is always true;
There were other times. We had other selves.
Now I remember how in slippers you padded
To our room, to turn out the gas light.
The small gashed globe went ember-red
And briefly smouldered on into the night.
As the purring faded our room regained
Its attic silence. And then you quietly came
To both our sides. You made the sign of Christ
Upon our sleepy heads. And said *God bless*.
Now in the greater darkness, the small light out,
Your clumsy, silent hands seem, almost, eloquent.

FF11506 Driver

Those who suffer in silence know no history.
Plato had a metaphor for it. Blindness,
Passivity of mind. He put us underground,
Hunched prisoners of the dark, watching dark
Shadows cast upon the dark. Exiled from the sun.
An absence of light. And no clear lineage.
Given the tabloid version, the TV image.
The cavern's shadows were always on the screen.
We'd no idea of who we were or who we'd been.
We went ashamed of what was rightly ours.
When relations died we burnt their personal things;
The photographs melted in the ash like tears.

Today I come across your driver's badge;
I grab it like a kleptomaniac.

The Singing Head

Harsh. And remote. A square for graves.
A mile from Sheringham. The coast road.
Wind warps the hawthorn. Dwarfs the pines.
Brine abruptly burns the memorial rose.
Mother mourns here, planting against the odds.
Over the inscribed slabs gulls rise and scream.
Singed petals scatter across the epitaphs.
The incoming sea's chopped white and green.

Orpheus' head churns in its own blood,
Shudders with each and every turbulence;
Battered, blind, it turns; bobs on the flood:
A severed head that will not sink,
But through the silence and the blood-stained rings
It sings—it sings—it sings—it sings—it sings.

Coda

The Buddha Statue

On the Downs they are burning the stubble;
Across the fields smoke clouds rise and billow.
Stalks and husks are being burnt to dust—
Even the last thin silk poppies have to go,
Surrender their scarlet to the black. I linger
At the edges, to turn the cold dank shards
Of memory, to word a further question.
Yet on the mantelpiece the Buddha statue stands.
His crowned head is an infolded flower;
His slim body a stem in the jug of being.
His dark body glimmers.
All through the annihilating
Motion of this day his hands are still.
Time turns upon itself. And spirals in.

Open to Change

Out from this rock, wind-worn, rain-razed
The Buddha stares into the bludgeoning storm;
The shrubs' roots crack open the dome of his mind;
The husks, bursting, break his woman's smile:
The death of the Buddha! And all patriarchs!
Yet he's composed; more tranquil now than when
His maker hacked him from intractable stone.
Soon blue butterflies will flit before him
And ants will crawl across those worn eyelids;
By his shoulders the leaves will burst their calyx
And unfold; green, yellow, shrivel and fade.
Beneath his gaze our lives betray themselves:
Broken, open to change. And the world turns
And turns. And the light burns. And the light burns.

From
Personae
1995

Prologue

This is not a text.
These words are not signs.
It does not concern race. Class. Gender.

This is not a silence on the page
Nor the latest Rorschach test
To prompt infantile rage or childhood trauma.

This is not a poem for contending critics.
Is not for the small margins of newspapers.
Is not a cultural resource. Not an entertainment. Not a learning
    aid.

This is a dispossessed cry which longs to know itself.
It starts. It stops. It hesitates.
It aches to grasp

Its shape, to own the promise of its anguish.
If it has a secret it would like accompaniment.
Hand-clap. Drum.

It breaks from the throat.
It tears the tongue. Is blood. Is scream. Is sound. Is word.
Is almost musical.

Song of Orpheus

I was the first in an unforgettable line.
Honoured. Then maligned. Inventor of the lyre.
Who failed Eurydice. Who raided the archives

Of the body. Found sex. Found death. Who from guilt
Made beauty. A lyric on the blood-soaked tongue.
Tested by fire, cleansed by water, absolved by it.

Who plucking the taut gut
Drew gulls. Drew rocks. Drew stones. Drew trees
Lumbering to the one bright edge. Who stalked

The labyrinth of bone. Who staggered through the hall
Of skulls. Who came back. Little to show:
Stark line, staccato sound, a broken cadence.

Who outsang the sirens,
Copywriters, entertainers, impresarios of a jaded time.
Whose one law is transformation.

Whose one rule is song. Who floats bleeding battered
On the tidal stream. A singing head
To calm the dizzy stars. Slow their cooling.

Fallen Man with one Wing

*Only the youngest brother, whose sleeve she had had no time to
finish, had a swan's wing instead of an arm . . .*

From the Grimms' *The Six Swans*

I'm a stranger here.
Have no parents. No clear past. No fixed address.
I am a catalogue of questions with only riddles
For answers. I limp boundaries, stumble through war-zones
Where history meanders, breaks off, locks on itself.
I struggle each day to keep two feet on the ground.
Death sticks in the palm of my hand like a hand-grenade.

From where did I fall? From what height to what depth?
What time was it then? Was it night? Were there stars
In the vault of the sky? Or was it the heart of day?
Were there strips of blue out over the sea?
Was anyone there? Did they record my fall?
All the bureaucratic forms, all the files are blank.
Then, who spun the garment which half covers my skin?
Who draped it over my head? It nettles and stings.

Amnesiac under the sun, the more I question
The less I understand. And what is this wing where
An arm should be? This shaming thing. This dark impediment.
And who put a star on my brutish brow
To mark me out for what inscrutable purpose?
It burns. I touch it. There's gold on my hand.
I'm on trial here. Much of the time I'm out
Of my mind. I scrawl notes when I can.

It is evening. The sun falls through amber.
We could be near the end of Winter.

In Defence of the Raven

And it came to pass at the end of forty days that Noah opened the
window of the ark which he had made: and he sent forth a raven,
which went forth to and fro, until the waters were dried up from off
the earth. Also he sent forth a dove.

Genesis Ch. 8 v. 6–8

It did not leave at once. For two hours
Or more it perched on the ark,
Eyeing the waves and the slanting horizon:
A dark witness under storm clouds.

Nor, when it finally left, did it go lightly.
At first, unsure of direction, it flew
Without grace. An equivocation of wings,
A mere inch above drowning water.

By all means cherish the dove. It returned
Loyally with good news in its beak.
So make it your icon on banners of peace
And hang them over the warring cities.

But, at night, as you try to sleep, remember
Far horizons, black holes, exploded nova stars;
Remember the curved edge of God's
Incommensurable mind—where the raven flies.

The Messiah

We had been waiting ever since we were born,
Crouched in the kitchen, where the ceiling flaked,
Or in the parlour with the curtains drawn—

As if home was the birth-place for a dread
That defied naming. The monologue of fear
Was in our eyes. Little was ever said.

Then as Spring was about to break each year,
A tall man arrived with a chalice of ash.
Thou art dust, he chanted in my ear,

And unto dust thou shalt return. With his thumb
He pressed the crumbling mark of Christ
Into our baffled flesh. My mind went numb.

We spent our lives with our knees on marble
In obscure corners with confessional voices
Heard just out of reach. Yet I was more than sure

We would be notified when the event came,
Receive an official letter giving a date
And a place, a number and a name.

Yet he arrived unannounced. A knock on the door
On another uneventful day and the Messiah
Stood there, smooth-shaved and assured.

We nodded. And assembled like children.
He told us to leave things as they were:
The kettle steamed into the air,

The dogs yelped and scratched at the door.
We lined up like cherubim.
It was the end we had been waiting for.

Rembrandt in Winter

The signature at the bottom of Self Portrait Aged 63 has
disappeared except for the letter 't'.

At sixty three, what matters now?
Death deals her signs.
Yet an unfamiliar light coruscates your brow,
Gutters and shines.

At the bottom corner of the frame
The darkness floods.
Of your illustrious baker's name
The 't' still floats

For Transience and Time which engulf all
Desperate strokes.
I sign my name because I'm mortal;
Born to pass.

Stranger, I wanted you to know that once,
Hands clasped together,
I faced myself. And with no chains of office,
In ice-cold weather,

Without furs or velvet hat or bronze breast plate
In a brown coat,
In the failing heart of winter, worked to place
Against the deficit

Some positive: my mind—mind's reflection—myself
At every move,
Watching experience unravel itself
Down to the spool.

Letter to Theo from his Brother: June 1889

I am incarcerated here at St Remy.
The maniacal sun hammers the small window.
All night I think of home: the North Sea

Pounding the flat land, the dykes, drained fields,
Where razor-winds squall and blow
Gashing the geometric and metallic waters.

Yet I plan to return. For, brother, my mind
Flounders. At times I no longer know
Who or what I am; and am unable to find

A way back. Like someone sensing the water cold
Struggles to regain the bank . . . I'll not go on. Theo,
Have any of my recent paintings sold

Or been talked of in Paris? It's oppressive here.
Gendarmes guard my work. The locals in the street
Turn their heads. The young kids point and stare

Coldly. I shall not now become what I might have been.
Please send more paint, all colours: cobalt,
Ultramarine, zinc, white, emerald green—

I'll daub against the darkness and in a trance
Render the sun. Cracked with voltages of blue
The plane trees rise into a yellow turbulence.

Weird forces break over me in waves.
I'll load the brush. And keep it true.
Artists are the broken vessels of their age.

Egon Schiele in Prison: April 1912

On 13th April 1912 the young painter Egon Schiele was suddenly, without explanation, put into prison at Neulenbach.

To hell with chiaroscuro! And what use
A thousand Grecian plaster casts when
My skin erupts with boils
And simmers at sexual boiling point?
Judge Savanorola there was bound to be
Misunderstanding between us. Even

When I was small you lumbered in
To burn my steam train sketches.
Art pollutes the hygiene of the mind
You said—or something like it;
And *Stick to academic subjects.*
My gangling limbs were strictly unclassical;

My appetite irregular. Here I gag with the stench
Of sweat, carbolic acid, excrement.
Some convict has gouged his initials
Deep into the wood. *MR April 1912.*
Six small leaves decorate a bone-like twig;
A spider dangles from its mangled web.

I am an insurrection of images desperate
For space. Incarcerated, I'm sick
For pencils, charcoal, brushes, paint.
I jam my fingers in my mouth and scrawl
The stations of the cross in phlegm and spit.
They stay ten seconds. Then evaporate.

Stanley Spencer's Beatitude

Each new fold in her skin appearing as her age increased was a new joy to him.

Stanley Spencer in his journal.

Half a century now, they've loved like this:
Violent. Urgent. Gentle. Shy.
He's come to her insatiably, more times
Than he can count, record or possibly
Remember. And now he watches her undress;
Once more, worships the whiteness of her flesh,
Straps and stays, eyes and hooks which press
Into her sagging skin leaving those pinkish
Stipples he desires to kiss, aching to have
Her grey hair between his wrinkled finger tips.
Old age has made their lust articulate.
I love your stuff inside me, she quietly says.
Wild, crumpled flowers, their faces touch and press.
And *yes,* he says. And *yes.* And *yes.* And *yes.*

Dante to Virgil at the Entrance to Hell

(After Canto III of the Inferno)
David Cook: *And what about Humanity?*
Alan Clark: *I'm not concerned with abstractions of that kind.*
12th November 1992 BBC 4

And so we came to that place unrecorded in books
Or maps; not found in archives or libraries.
The night smouldered without stars. At times
It was so dark I could see nothing. On all sides
There rose gagged screams, muffled sighs:
A mixture of filth, insinuation, jargon, lies.
Be economical with the truth, one says. Another cries
Humanity? What is that? Tears pricked my eyes.
And all the time a blizzard scoured the place;
A million grains of sand blistered my face.
Master, I said, *For Christ's sake who are these men?*
The answer came at once. *They are the nation's scum,*
Which rises quickly. They are maggots that worm
Their way through venison. Survivors, to the end;
Who learning the art of words become the masters of deceit;
Yet are always silent when it serves them well.
Observe them closely. For we are at the entrance into hell.
It was then I saw that banner whipping the wind,
Zig-zagging as it swirled, now *Left,* now *Right,*
Now *Low,* now *High.* Such a mob followed on—
Who would have thought Death had undone so many?
From their blotched faces blood streamed to the ground
Where bloated worms rose up, to gulp it down.

The Love Song of Peter Abelard

*When inspiration did come to me it was for writing love-songs, not
the secrets of philosophy.*

I want the conjunction of your looks,
Not the declension of nouns in monastic cribs;
I want the time back I mangled on books.

I want your laughter to explode in my ears;
I want the babble of your monosyllabic words;
I want your eyes moist with their singular tears.

I want the advanced theology of your finger tips,
The gravitas of your breasts against my ribs;
I want your wisdom to slide under my lips.

I want that dark delta where rivers congregate,
Where lunar tides rock in and out;
Where the flat sea, like spilt silver, stretches out.

Emily Dickinson's Declaration

She came to me with two day lilies and said:
'These are my introduction'.

Dear stranger—take this lily—
It has the aroma
Of sex
And death—

A formality
Few plants possess—
Its green stem
Is virginity—

Its white flower
Consciousness—
Stranger—
Honour its singularity—

Do not sell my witness
In the market place—
Permit no barter—
But set it—rather—

In a blue vase—
In a disused chapel—
On a distant hill—
Under the violent stars—

D.H. Lawrence's First Lesson: The Apple

Let the apple be X: The Elements of Algebra Book I.

Dear student, you have my permission.
Create a revolution, if you must,
But only for the fun of it; not for social class,

Nor cash. And, whatever you do,
Continue to resist the text.
Do not let the apple be X.

Now clear away your books.
As I place this apple on your desk
Look at its freckled skin;

Observe its mellow creases, its curving lines.
See with your own clear eyes
The beauty of its blemishes.

Now touch its gloss and sheen.
Next taste the flesh, sense Autumn on your tongue,
The sourness vying with the sweetness:

A long white second of communion.
This is what you know, and this is best.
This is the Alpha and the Omega—

Before the little X.

What God will you do?

Developed from a conception of Rilke's.

What, God will you do when I am dead?
I am your vase. What if I am carelessly broken?
I am the clay vessel which carries your drink.

Where, God will you be when I am dead?
I am your listening ears; I am your glancing eyes.
I am your tongue through which you taste your earth.

How will you mature when I'm not there?
For I am your evolving language. I stutter your conceptions.
I utter your immense feelings.

I'm your prayer. What will you do without me?
What will you do without your scribbling messenger?
Will you continue blind and alone?

God, I am your dramatist. When the play is over
I fear the silence and see only desert,
Where appalling winds rake the sand, for ever.

This Head

I woke with this marble head in my hands.
George Seferis

Between my hands this ancient head, unclaimed.
I picked it up in a shocking dream
And could not put it down again. Half-crazed
Curator, I want it to be seen.

Its eyes stare into a radiance beyond our grasp;
Its face peels with burning skin.
Though it may desire to speak to us,
A fastidious mouth shuts it in.

I will ransack archives, break gummed seals,
Crack open vaults, desecrate graves
To find its world and speak for him.
Two lives are over. A third begins.

New Constellations

One often hears: that is good but it belongs to yesterday. But I say:
yesterday has not yet been born. It has not really existed. I want Ovid,
Pushkin and Catullus to live once more.

Osip Mandelstam.

You do not begin alone; rather, you extend
A narrative. Through the half-open window
The breeze blows in spiked with salt
And distance. Your senses stir until
Your memories rise into new constellations.
Who said that there can be no more beauty? That art
Must be minimal or brutal: an ideological aid
Or bare reflection—a mirror laid across
A gallery floor. Or some such dull cleverness?
The mind's traffic jams in the maze of the sign,
Ironic civilisation silts and chokes itself.
These words lie dark on the field of the page:
Hard, obdurate grains against the age.

The past, which never truly was, returns again.

From
Angelic Imagination
1997

In the Beginning

In the beginning was the Word.
It became flesh.
It walked amongst us.
It stuttered its own meaning.
It was its own enigma.
It spoke in paradox.
It dreamed.

It was not comprehended.
It was cornered by questions.
It was crowned with thorns.
It was nailed to a tree.
It tasted vinegar.
It was pierced through the side.
It screamed.

It was placed in a tomb.
It came back.
It was Word again.
It uttered its distilled meanings.
It was Song.
It was free.
It redeemed.

A Tempest for our Times

Ariel is no longer here. Her spirit
Dissolved into thin air, the vaguest kind
Of memory now. Did she ever flit
Through our intactable world for love of mind?
But Caliban's back! He's come up triumphant,
A disc-jockey in a silk suit, pimp
Of the mega-machine. He grunts at us
In monosyllables and grins at his luck.
And Prospero? Senex and Mage he sits
Through this interminable committee-meeting,
Stats and facts at ten finger-tips:
To report back *in due course, when, etcetera.*

Lights to dim until it is so dark
The absence of light in dark can be discerned.

On Seeing Vermeer's Kitchen-Maid in the Rijksmuseum

For Miranda

It arrests you as you stroll until you reel,
Almost breathless, dizzy with the thing seen.

Monumental in dark blues and yellows—
The maid stands steadying a household jug.

The white milk flows from vessel to vessel.
World thickens. Time bulks. Breath slows.

Crowds pass—cameras snap—guides give their spiel.
But you must stand here alone, seeing and unseen.

On the table before her, unbroken loaves;
Behind her ineffable light floods in.

Artist's Manifesto

For Lynne Gibson

The artist detonates his mind to let in God's.
Under his loaded brush the world ignites.

Perception burns to vision. Metaphysics
Dance in his eyes. Under his finger-tips

All life's transmutation, an alchemist's laboratory
For experiments. Oh!—to set the imagination free

In the hard crucible of nature, to begin
To murder fate, to let the incandescent angel in!

The Shadow on Bonnard's Face

Hard on himself, haunted, self-effacing,
He stoops before us, reticent. And questioning.
A shadow darkens the length of his face.
Can this be Bonnard who affirms our place
As modern alchemists and brought Paradise
To the Villa du Bosquet? Painting after painting
Where seeing is sacramental and metaphysics
Carnal as wine, as red as apples ripening
On a white cloth, blue as the sea's distance.
And Martha sets his imagination free.
Hour after hour she baths for him—God's
Voyeur! Even the dead tiles change their hues;
Resurrect in greens, yellows, ochres, blues—
A surplus for the goddess as the water cools.
And then this shadow darkening across his face.

Intimations of Mortality

Late November and the first frosts are cleansing
This place. There are gaps in the trees;
Irregular holes in the fence. The neighbours
Are incinerating the leaves

And I imagine myself not here.

The flames poke through the shrivelled heaps;
Last month's decapitated heads disappear
In thin meandering smoke. It drifts across
The boundary into our home

And I imagine myself not here.

Today the frosted lawn is a beautiful
Altar cloth, starched and crisp, and laid out
For no god. The pond is a sheet of glass;
It returns the sky. Immaculate. Blue. Silent. Vast.

Too near to Death

You have been too near to death too long;
In the silent cancer wards watching lives,
Once beautiful and loud with hope, decay;
And now you stand alone, huge with grief

And inconsolable. So much undone.
So much you did not know. Nor do. Nor say.
Minute particles of grief lie on every book
And photograph; and on every random wind

A dry incriminating dust blows in.
At each door in every corridor
Promiscuous death stands with his letcher's grin -
And life's the calamity no-one talks about.

Psalm

After Paul Celan

No-one can create us again out of the dust.
No-one.

Never.

Hallowed be thy name, No-one.
Who is not in heaven.

Not the Power.

Nor the Glory.

For your sake
We live and flower.

We are not roses—
Our stamens broken,
Our stems blood red.

Not in the beginning.

Nor in the end.

Flowering now and for never.
Without

Amen.

Angelic Imagination

A Poem in Five Movements
In Memory of Kate Cooper: Young Composer

1

Child, your blonde locks gone,
    bald-headed,
        involuntary Buddha
you walk among us
    prematurely wise. Your nine
        brief years
make our more casual time
    seem mean
        and almost criminal.
On an unseen boundary line
    you hover and dance,
        a recorder at your lips;
Allegro and *Andante* arch,
    absurdly beautiful, above
        the savagery of chance.
Stranded in safer places we are
    your sad and
        feckless witnesses
as now you fight your failing lungs
    for one more
        blast of breath-
to blow a final cadence
    of beauty
        against your death.

2

Almost a spectre now, still
   whispering *yes*, wanting
      the shamanic flute
for the hesitant breath.
   At each blow life,
      brief and equivocal,
blossoms at the stem.
   Dear mortal child how
      you defy
the body's cancerous duplicity.
   From the plenitude
      of sound
an ultimate simplicity.
   So promiscuous Death
      give over!
Beyond all trauma her breath
   hurls out its
      musical hosanna.

3

Dear child, my darling Orpheus,
   you have called on Death
      and heard its pitiless *No*
and now return to play for us
   Andante and *Allegro*. Fearless,
      you walk a lonely isthmus
between rising tides,
   music at your lips, recorder
      in your hands.

Where squalling wind is deaf and
    staring ocean blind,
        your *allegro* rises up,
pierces the distraught mind.
    The music mounts
        the hostile air
and almost heals. And almost mends.
    Spirit begins
        where nature ends.

4

Who comes at noon who
    waits in doorways
        lingers in the afternoon
who stammers who smiles who
    teases who burns deceit
        who scorches ease
who runs between the slanting rain
    who answers gulls who
        scrawls her name
under their wild white wings
    who is the lexicon of love
        the syntax of tears
who is the freight of dreams
    who disappears who
        returns with Orpheus
whose music rises as breath
    fragrant as memory
        as intangible as death.

5

(After Rilke)

Raise no commemorative stone.
   Roses shall blossom
      all summer for her sake—
for she is Orpheus whose change
   of key is magical
      and constant.
Fatuous to ask nature for its reasons.
   Once and for all:
      Where there's music
She's there. Her urgent call
   transfigures
      and turns to dust
the plastic wreaths and slogans.
   It's hard for us
      to grasp transcendence.
Even Orpheus dreads that moment
   when she must move
      beyond us-
Yet when her hand slips from
   the quivering instrument
      there's no subterfuge
and nothing's superfluous.
   Angelic imagination
      vaults to its freedom.

The Night Journey

For Theodore

Go down these steps but enter slowly.
The door opening cuts a rectangle of light.
A dark room. A hidden labyrinth underground.

Earth's smell clamps nose and throat;
The vaulted silence takes my breath away.
Weren't you ever told this place was out of bounds?

When the next door opens a faded, cobwebbed, light
Breaks through. An orange butterfly flits across.
Can you remember it now? Does it come back?

Slowly it returns. The aroma of honey coating the dust—
And all that bee-keeping paraphernalia:
The long white vestments, the black-meshed hoods,

Those glinting containers, those silver drums,
A liquid gold dripping from their sticky taps—
The jam-jars brim-full of the golden stuff;

Then up three steps and slowly out,
Squinting into the light of an ordinary day,
The sun dropping behind the charcoal woods.

And what does it all mean to you now? Can you say?
I imagine substances growing in the dark beneath.
Alchemical. Strange. Silent. Out of reach.

From
Love after Sappho
1999

Post-Modern Love

I do not know what way to move; I am of two minds.

—SAPPHO

Incomparable Beauty

Once more, incomparable beauty burns my skin.
I am a delta of fire.
Aphrodite loosen my limbs!

Who said there could be no more love poetry?
For each day some-one, somewhere,
Falls into love's vortex. Is half dismembered,

Half encompassed there. Chill douses his spine,
Sweat glues his hair. And all around
Swirls apprehension. A man, near drowning, dreads

The depth of the water he no longer treads. To compare
It to the nakedness of birth, the completeness
Of death, the radiance of gods is hardly to start.

It is the long insomniac nights, tears
Jagging the eyes, the stammering heart.

First Fall-Out

We woke early and on the window saw this labyrinth:
Seeded ferns, feathered grass, bridges.

Love, you said, this is our looking-glass.
This is our ancient city and our inner maze.
The story of our lives is written here.

But as we gazed the sun came up
A blistering and a burning orange.
It melts our world, dissolves our city—

And all the names we whispered; *fern, grass,*
Bridge, dome, spire, pyramid slide down the glass
Like tears—like pain—like Hiroshima—like Nagasaki.

Our kissing now is cruel and bitter.
First Fall-Out. First Nuclear Winter.

Kamikase Stars

Brutal in the heart of August winter slips in,
Strips the green foliage, burns the green leaves.
Cool on my brow. Cold on your fingers.

An oil drum flares without a sound.
Pyramids of skulls rise from the smoking ground.
A war-lord patrols his cardboard town.

Insubstantial ghost I pace the wooden floor.
What for? What ultimately for?
Our lacerating days go out like all the others.

The guru in the Book of Wisdom speaks:
Throw the dice twice—then leave it to the play of chance.
The kamikase stars blaze into the infinite.

Divided lovers, where are we?
Under the smouldering rubble. Under the burning sea.

A Bleeding Wreath

Now we stare both ways across the divide,
Lonely together, paradoxical, Janus-eyed.
There's no holding back the jagged tide—

Its salt-serrated edges, its undertow, its minute
By minute, fierce ebbing back and out.
We shiver as we kiss, drown as we doubt.

Our age is a tip of abandoned faiths. Nothing's secure;
The currents are murderous on this modern shore—
They have taken other drifting lives before

With no disgorging of the bodies from their depths;
And there are no gods left to lay a bleeding wreath
For the sundering of marriage—suddenness of death.

Las Vegas Perhaps

There's this city I am driving to. Las Vegas—
Perhaps. Its gaudy beads of light seduce,
Release adrenalin. I'm in a stolen car
And travelling fast. Suddenly, it blows a tyre.
The vehicle somersaults, bursts into fire.
I scramble out—my hair's ablaze—and shout—
For Christ's sake help. The traffic neither stops
Nor brakes. The drivers turn their ghostly heads—
And then accelerate . . . Love, there are no words
For dreams like this. They detonate the mind.
Where was I running from?
What was I running for?
This numbing loss—this age-old fear.
Tell me I still exist . . . Stroke my burning hair.

Under the Burning Sycamore

We walk through the autumn wood. Time is the cadence
Of our falling steps, the rhythm of our passing.
What can assuage our transience—

So briefly breath condenses in the air. Shrivelled leaves
And twigs lodge in our clothes and streaming hair.
The Buddha says *All things pass.*

Work on your life with diligence. When did he say these words?
Under what forsaken tree? And when did we stroll into
The smouldering wreckage of this wood?

Memories break, fade, go slack. Chrysanthemums shed
Their dark aroma; their crowns are packed with death.
A silence beats against my head

Its chill amnesia. We are spindrift prone to dream,
Our hours cremating into ash. Under the burning sycamore
The blackbird sings our requiem.

Pisces

We draw our astrological sign on sand
As the brackish tide comes in, crass lovers,
Imagining the world as ours—as if our hand
Could map love onto the burning planets,

Black holes, imploding stars. *In the beginning
A vast explosion. An incomparable violence.*
Then who are we? And where do we fit in?
Creatures of chaos, quirks of chance.

Our astrological signs are sealed and coded songs;
They cannot disclose the purpose of the galaxies,
Nor grace this barren shore. Ceaseless tongues
Of salt erase our zodiacal scrawl.

Only inside our fraying lives these marks are more,
Unbounded surplus—not maps, but metaphor.

Descendants of the Fireball

Let me gaze upon the candour of your face,
Beautiful after so much grief, and trace
Again your body's braille. Under intent
And moving finger-tips our lives seem eloquent—

Yet we stare down a contracting cone of time:
Man. Mammal. Mollusc. Amoeba. Slime.
Vast explosion. Unbridled violence.
And who are we in this ungentle universe?

Nothing returns our scanning gaze. Do we exist
To amaze ourselves, to leap the distance
Of the galaxies? *To cancel—to transcend!*
Even as we speak an exploding star sends

Light into an infinity no-one can read, nor comprehend.
Let us burn brightly against our end.

Jewels of Consciousness

Love, listen—we exist to surpass ourselves,
To break the boundaries of our cells, *to cancel—*
To transcend! Nothing in nature tells us
Who we are. Consider the music of the spheres—
Random blips, distant howls, inhuman blurs.
Planets collide . . . Huge stars explode . . .
Black holes devour matter . . . Quasars implode.
Nature's a terrorist who enters fast. She decrees
The law of entropy to every part,
Scrubs clean the archives of the brain, with no heart,
For no purpose, for no God, for no justifying art—
Blots out memory, annuls the past.
So who are we in all of this? Small, dazzling
Jewels of consciousness—against the dark.

Speaking of Eros

Gilded, you said, they were gilded by love;
It was as if when they smiled the gods above
Poured honey over them. Their limbs were gold
And shone transparent. As you spoke a cold

Sweat broke over me. I knew if I had the power
I would have had them executed in the public square,
Hung, drawn, quartered or crucified upside down,
Their honeyed limbs dragged over common ground—

And would have shredded all lies in their defence,
For ease of civilization requires a formal reticence.
Then later came those swarming flies—
Buzzing through my mouth, my ears, my socket-eyes.

At Cuckmere Estuary

We stand on the shingle as night comes in. Behind us
Storm clouds, bruised and red, slump to the Downs. This is
The last violence of the haemorrhaging sun. Lightning forks

And flickers vertical at the edge. All that our eclectic times
Have claimed dissolves. We listen to a silence whose signs
Are hard and hazardous to read. We are novices. New-comers.

Inland a siren wails and spreads its shrill alarm. At last
The stillness returns, more intensely reticent for the dissonance.
The reason is ... The reason is ... There are no reasons left;

Platitudes jostle in the gaps. The healing word takes flight
In the daily battle-ground of microphones and hype;
And singing Orpheus drowns in a flood of camera light.

A Mantra of Accidental Light

Time has no purpose, but you come again
To grace my life. Love's jaded jargon cries
On my tongue, bitter with past betrayals,
Ancient battles, festered scars, tabloid lies.

Love's a plastic tag on merchandise
And Eros a pornographer. Under every word
An angel bleeds, dragged from the arching sky,
And raped and blinded. Cupid, you have become

A crazed, degraded thing—a crass hard-on
For every predilection. Who now can speak of
Love's celestial influence? Today I return
Your steadfast glance without a word.

The furnace sun is bronze upon your hair.
A mantra of accidental light. A form of prayer.

A Violent Cleansing

We woke last night to hear the bitter rain
Scouring the slates, flaying the window pane,
Flooding the dark river. After a long dry spell
Such a savage cleansing. And as we fell
Into uneasy sleep, I sensed the driven rain
Wash our sprawling polluted cities clean.
A single ablution through the slow black hours.
A brute force, the wind rampaged the streets
Clawing the seductive eyes, the simulated smiles,
The glittering masks of affluence—while
A pitiless icy rain erased the lexicon
Of power, insidious betrayals, soft jargon.
Love, when the new dawn's morning breaks
With pristine beauty, do not rush to speak.

Navigating Darkness

Sometimes I think of us: obscure spiders
Spinning from our entrails metaphysical webs,
Acrobats who hang from a single thread

Dancing awkwardly to silk the sullen emptiness,
To weave together disparate things, leaf and ledge,
Branch and bridge, the vital and the dead.

Our fragile geometries shimmer over the abyss.
Or sometimes I see us through another image:
That athletic girl on a warm Minoan hill;

Upside down, she somersaults the charging bull—
A red speck of transcendence against the blue.
A mere child. Inviolable. Free. And falling still.

And then I think of Sappho: *the lightest breath*
Yet my words live on—in the acoustic chambers
Of our mind, navigating darkness beyond the stars.

Last Rites

But all must be endured.

—Sʌᴘᴘʜᴏ

At Cromer Hospital

Mother, I sit powerless by your bed.
Crouched under newly laundered sheets,
Your body has shrunk to that of a child.
Your face is cracked, eyes blue as cornflowers.
You shouldn't have come all that way to see me,
I'm alright . . . A few days left to live, self-effacing
As ever. Though you can barely lift a child's
Beaker to your lips, you ask for barley water.
The drip-feed's off; there'll be no more solids.
Once, I'd have done anything for you;
A timid boy, I loved you to excess.
Outside the ward June's burning laburnum
Spills on the world a fading radiance.
The morphine zips in to ease the dying.

All Night in Hospital

All night in hospital I hold your hand
And ache to sleep. Unread newspapers litter
The room. Unwanted food, unwanted drink
Stand on the window sill. Here time neither ticks
Nor moves, but hangs silent and oppressive.
A patient in another ward screams out—a flurry
Of movement—a metal trolley clatters down
An unseen corridor. In an urgent track of time
Someone, somewhere, is dying. Almost dawn.
Outside the senile day begins. Birds repeat
Their morning platitudes, blank clouds gather.
Grotesquely the sun breaks through. Mother,
What can we place against such huge indifference?
A hand across the skull. Love's glance. This breath.

Travelling to a Foreign Land

And now flowers in their glass vases burn
With furious incandescence. Red. Yellow.
Blue. Absurdly beautiful.
I hold your frail veined hands.
Put vaseline on your lips, lavender water
On your brow. Our final ritual. You slip
Into sleep, stir, start to hallucinate.
Strange animals stalk the place. Silver spoons
Rise in the room and then, an oracle, you speak;
Feelings are hard to portray . . . You must understand
The other view . . . It's like travelling to a foreign land.
Mother, I have never heard you quite so eloquent.
I squeeze your hands and kiss your dried out lips—
As the vessel of our lives drifts to the precipice.

Extreme Unction

Today the priest arrives. He holds the crucifix
For you to kiss. He makes the sign of Christ
Upon your frowning brow, your dried-out lips.
I stand awkward. I cannot kneel nor say
Amen ... As a child I prayed for life eternal;
Now life dissolves under our finger-tips.
We lurch to our extinction. And die alone.
This is the poison which blisters the skin;
This is the chemical which corrodes the bone.
Holy Mary, Mother of God, pray for us
Sinners now and at the hour of our death—
At the end of taste—at the end of touch—
At the end of speech—at the end of breath—

At the Old House

Last night I slept at the old house alone.
Half ghost, half insomniac, I thought
Of all the wasted hours we spent there,
Uncut, unharvested, unbound.
What was I hoping for? A moment to gather in
The stunted crop? Memory gave little back.
Outside a blank moon hurtled through the black.
Today I visit your unsettled grave.
The wreaths have gone, their flimsy ribbons
Lie on the earth, silk-blue and shimmering.
What else remains? A scorched rectangle of turf
Where a cavity had been, a nameless ache
Beneath the aching skin, no clear horizon.
An implacable sky, a growing emptiness within.

On Sheringham Beach

I walk today's decaying line of flesh and bone:
How to redeem the mean apotheosis of time,
The endless drift, the detritus and waste?
Here at seventeen I strolled reciting Hopkins
To the waves, Wordsworth's poems in my pocket—
A talisman against the age. I was drunk on words,
Dizzy on their arcs of sound.
What time brings time terminates.
On the promenade old men eye the altercations
Of the tide. It daily rises to withdraw
And spews its dead upon the shore.
Above the casual slaughter the sky recedes
Into a blank infinitude where gulls,
Like apparitions, scream—then drop into oblivion.

A Girl in Sepia

Mother, there's still a bitterness on my tongue
And iron rusts near my heart. It's hell
To speak the truth. With you, I seldom did.
Absurdly shy, I was the kind of child who stared
And stuttered, to find long after the event the words
He hungered for. Tonight I look through photographs;
Here you are, a girl—in sepia—your First Communion:
All curls and frills. And here you are—in black and white—
Eighteen. Young. And vulnerable. And beautiful.
And here decades later—in Kodak colour—
The small, huddled, stubborn woman I remember.
I still wince before your flawed, excessive love;
Yet now, far too late, beyond the grave,
Ache to thank you—for the life you gave.

The Dance of Syllables

Come my holy lyre
Find your voice and speak to me.

—Sᴀᴘᴘʜᴏ

Alchemists Down the Age

This is the beginning of a poem. It is a vessel
For disparate things. Each day brings an element,
Unclassified, raw, incalcitrant. Car crash,

A burning head, glass. The lilac massing purple
At the window, a word in the discarded paper,
Stray threads of a marriage. Blood. Coriander. Ash.

Then the power's switched on. Flames lick the flask,
Blacken the base. Nothing's clear but the task;
The stirring, testing, tasting—that slow thickening

As the heat rips. What is it that I'm after?
An enduring amalgam that fuses the parts.
Was this the labour for gold? The philosopher's ring?

I think of alchemists down the age, god's poets—
Artisans working through the insomniac hours—
With burnt fingers, charred skin, cracked hands.

The Naming of Things

Intimate stranger, I name for you what things I can:
Demotic daisy, prophetic dandelion,

Jasmine, freesias, acanthus, saxifrage,
A litany of scattered names

Plucked from the hurricane of riven time,
Syllables to set against oblivion.

Their cadence rides our urgent breath
Flowering before the void of death.

Yet who can restore, what can atone
The melanoma of skin, the necrosis of bone,

Alzheimers, cancer of doubt,
Sudden unmeaning, slackening, the blackening out?

Bewildered naming in the thick of time:
Demotic daisy. Prophetic dandelion.

Sprigs of Rosemary

I bring this sprig of rosemary; but what is rosemary for?
It is for releasing memory, for increasing memory's store.

Yet few memories come back; childhood oppresses
With its weight of sullen fears. My life regresses

Into the black. I cannot remember what I said or did.
A haphazard crow flies at an angle to the wood.

So many memories gone into the gap under the falling wave,
Ash to the metallic fire, the blankness of the grave.

There's a paradox here. I pluck rosemary to mark what's absent,
To acknowledge what is over with aromatic scent,

To let it go with grace—and then I remember images of you:
The lapis lazuli against the whiteness of your neck, your sigh

At the eternal candour of its blue. You are the one somewhere
In my imagination with sprigs of rosemary in her hair

And sprays of bay leaves in her hands, whose radiant eyes
Bring back, at memory's furthest root, the glint of paradise.

The Aura of your Face

Who can describe the aura of your face?
A proof of the existence of God? Perhaps.
Today the sun's vertical light descends as grace

Through towering clouds to enlighten our late
Estrangement and I recall those Chinese paintings,
Long landscape scrolls, where in the firmament

Through rising scrawls of mist a small tree
Hangs over the abyss to blossom there—suddenly
White, frail, incomparable. *Imago dei.*

Massage

When your hands with a delicacy all their own
Hovered over my skin, caressing the dark hair,
Yielding to the hardness of cartilage and bone,

I remembered my father in his brief old age,
Sour with self-loathing, hawking into the stove
Soft black mucus. In the incomprehensible cage

Of his marriage, a wounded animal, love's pariah,
Padding the hard floor, sniffing the medical air,
Alone and fearing the beginning of nowhere.

And I wept for the touch he had never known,
The hand easing the skin, soothing the terminal bone:
The panther, uncaged, in its darkness coming home.

A White Dark-Scented Rose

Love, listen to these words that run obliquely,
That never quite declare their aim, nor yield
What they appear to promise. Strange. Haunted.

Labile. Remember, last night, how the dark wind
Blew the transfiguring snow across the Downs
Over the familiar dusty paths? Like that, but not

Like that at all. Or imagine a white dark-scented rose
In some unknown garden, petal by petal, silently
Opening, silently closing, and no God watching.

Like that, but not like that at all. These words
Rise on their cadence. They cast a further spell
Until we enter an estrangement which feels like home.

Love's Unicorn

Somewhat after Rilke

It never was. It never ran through tall grass.
It never tasted ice water on its tongue.
It never felt the salt wind nipping the nape of its neck.
It never saw the whiteness of its body.
It never was. It could never be.

Then, one day, you longed for its existence.
Slowly it emerged, intangibly it came.
It moved in the shadows, hovered in the undergrowth.
Its nostrils quivered, its clean eyes opened—
As if waiting for you to call its name.

And suddenly you said the secret word: *unicorn!*
A single horn broke from its stark brow.
Startlingly white. Precise. Spiralling to a point.
Ah! It existed then—in the silver mirror of your longing.
And that which never was, became.

Girl with a Flute

I think today of Osip Mandelstam at the edge
Of his charred life, pacing the streets of Voronezh,
A scorched bird locked in an iron cage,
Small head, tilted back, screaming his rage:
I am the tree-splitting storm—rain zig-zagging the glass—
The gargoyle frothing with water—Dante, Villon, Mozart—
The open mouth of God. Drawn to they know-not-what
The town kids jeer and shout: *General! General!*
But soon they will be mouthing his satirical songs,
His anti-Soviet doubt, his musical codas—
Each poem a mantra of defiant breath
Against the status quo, against his martyr's death.
What to think now? What cause should one salute?
A cadence in the wind. A girl with a flute.

The Marriage of True Minds

Jan van Eyck painted the Arnolfini Marriage in 1434.
For Annabel and Matthew

Here married love is memorable. It has the clarity
Of light filling a Dutch interior to announce
The virtues of the real, grace in what is ordinary.
This candelabra. This bed. Four ripe oranges.
Consider the movement of the bridegroom's hands:
How the right one is raised as if to bless,
While the left reaches out to reassure—
A marriage of seriousness and tenderness.
And the encompassing pattern of their love
Is everywhere: the dark green of the wedding dress
Against the red, one flickering candle above
Their temperate heads, the shaggy terrier at their toes.
And the convex mirror on the distant wall,
A lover's gazing eye, reflects it all.

The Dance of Syllables

Love, what is it that makes us listen
So intently? As if after so much history—
Denial, loss, desolation—there could
Be tongues of fire again, crimson scrawls
Of revelation. Not in the march of Progress
But in the dance of syllables . . . They enter
The ear's portals, the skull's cathedral
To fill the bare aisles, the gutted chapels,
The sad centres of our dereliction. For words
Do not refer to this world easily, yet
They have their music. Surplus. Fierce excess
Feeding the spirit where we live most freely—
Hovering over fathomless depths.
Out of reach. Torn. Stripped. Flying breathless.

The Song of Words

Water cleans itself until each amber stone
Shines beneath the turbulence: clear, angular,
Eloquent. Even ancient rock and slate and bone

Now yield their natural reticence to chant
The power of water, to sing its lilting essence:
Sa la sa la liea siea—all the way to the distant

Estuary, the jade cormorant, gull's clamour.
We utter more than we can ever know
For words like water crave the sea, flow under

Our intimate breath, slip under the ticking clock,
Sing in the eyes of the skull, rill in the jaws
Of death, the white spume gashing the rock:

Sa la sa la sa la
Liea siea

From
Viva la Vida
2005

Child of Pisces

Falling like Gulls

I often go at night to the top of that dust track
Looking for the storage place. I open the door to face
The dark. It's still aromatic with apples. Cool. Quiet.
On my way down the slatted shelves are on the right.
There's no ripening fruit laid out. But silence.

I pass to the Onion Shed. The wooden door rides on
Its runners jerkily—as it always did. Through the rectangle,
Chicken-wire, windows an opaque light filters in.
Ghostly. White. The bronzed onions we rolled along the boards
Have gone. Our children's shouts are silent in the wall.

I come to the Old House. I go down the green corridor.
The fire burns in the hearth. There's a book on the floor,
It's open on a blank. Outside there's a misty light.
The gate sags in the grass, the fields dip to the sea—
Where silent gulls rise momentarily. Then drop from sight.

Head Gardener

For my grandfather

Back bending to the ground, almost anonymous,
You could pass this place and hardly notice him;

A figure in a garden of espaliated pears, wallflowers,
Asparagus, broccoli. Silent connoisseur of soils

Crumbling in his hands the unseen filaments, cysts, spores:
A lump of clay breaking into life, the dull charisma of years.

But not only here, I see him on long summer afternoons
Alone in the hot glinting greenhouse, his pragmatic fingers

Rubbing the earth to a tilth, then funnelling the countless seeds
From their small dry packets into moist runnels.

Then some evenings, a handkerchief draped over his eyes,
I catch him in the arm-chair, his book slipping from his knees,

Those lean hands still at last—and I imagine all that seed
Germinating in the dark. Clean white shoots. Nubs of green.

Aspen Leaves

As I drift down, almost asleep, I am at the Oak Woods
Pushing the chipped blue door until it opens
Into the walled garden. Box-hedge greens the cinder paths;

They go to the deep pond. In the silver sheen small fish
Rise and fall, the shadows of aspen leaves. I hear the bees
Buzz against the dusty slate, taste the ripe peach's

Sweet pulp on my tongue, see the line of green beech
Opening into the fields, the gleam of the furrowed sea,
That far horizon. In a single instant—all within my reach.

But then the summer light fades fast and grandfather
Sits silent in his chair and the fire is all but out and there's
A handkerchief over his eyes and his book has fallen to the floor

And I'm running up the stairs and there's no light from the moon
And there's a wind gusting under the eaves
And then a hush and—only leaves and leaves and leaves.

Grandmother Reading at Myrtle Cottage

Sleepless—and I see you sitting there at the window,
Light fading as you settle to the pages
Of *The Methodist Recorder*.

Behind you the cavernous black of the back-room. The wood fire
Flickers, ignites the mahogany bureau and chairs
With splinters of orange and red.

You are doing the crossword and musing over passages
From the Bible: exile of Adam and Eve,
Murder of Cain, Jehovah's testing of Abraham,

The Exodus. You know these story-lines better than the lines
On the palms of your hands;
The Act of Creation right down to the moment you fill

The blank squares with a quotation
From the Psalms. In less than an hour it will be inexpungibly dark
And you will have slumped in the chair, and the answers

Slipped to the floor, then only irregular breath—
And the tick-tock-tick of the clock and nothing and nowhere.

The Glass Dome of Childhood

Almost a revelation this morning—the barn owl in the shopping
    mall,
Perching on a gloved hand, clawing the simulated leather.
I was drawn at once to its primitive power, its sheer presence.
Its fine wings quivered and shuddered in the fluorescent glare

Of the cramped precinct. I fell for the fall of its white feathers—
The wings like priest's vestments tapering into yellow and orange.
Its eyes hypnotised mine with their circles of primeval darkness.
I imagined the bird navigating the wildest night, its beak open,

Its claws fast, a daemon of terror, or wavering on rounded wings
In the dazzling trauma of some car's lights. Then I remembered
Another owl. It stood paralysed on a painted bough, lifeless
In the glass dome of my childhood. A hesitant boy I longed

To smash the polished glass, take the victim in my hands
And ease it through the windows into a healing sky—
And now that owl was fluttering before my open eyes,
Splaying its shamanic wings, emitting its long-caged cries.

A Catholic Childhood

After Antonio Machado

Late afternoon. A long shadow
Across the playground.
The dark thickens against the window
Without a sound.

We crouch as the priest strides
Between the wooden desks.
He asks: *why did God make us?*
This is our weekly Catholic test.

We chant the answer back:
God made us to know Him,
To love Him and to serve Him
And to be happy with Him forever

In the Next. A child of excess
I want to burn into his Name,
To melt into his side,
To dance into flame.

Any moment a miracle—
A voice from the dead,
A revelation from the timber roof,
Christ's oracular head.

Late afternoon. Outside a long shadow
Across the playground.
Light thickens against the window
Without a sound.

The White Gull's Beatitude

Each day, up at six, pale seminary boys, we walked compliant.
Our cells in shadow, the cloisters grey. *Morning Prayers.*
Meditation. Mass. That tyrannical god entering our mouths at the
    tinkling

Of a bell: Christ melting on our bridled tongues. I watched
The dark-robed priests, giant rooks garbling their Latin *Kyrie,*
And felt strangely aghast. I could not help thinking of that novice

Who on our first day had run for it along the sand to Liverpool,
Over the stench of fish, tarred wings, wreckage—salt anointing
    his skin,
The white gulls wheeling above his head yelping his beatitude

In the terror of his freedom. *Let him be anathema.* But I longed
To be like him, to claim the natural surge of courage, to serve
An open god, to sprint forever into some cloud-burst horizon.

Although I could not put a name to him, although he stood
A heretic condemned, he became my saint and icon,
One of my dissenting kind. Yet I lacked his impetuosity . . . I
    stayed on—

Aping the mumbling priests, a poor ventriloquist trying to conform.
Daily I mouthed the pallid prayers, lisped the theology by rote,
The bleached abstractions sticking like fish-bones in my throat.

Other Gifts

From my father the pang of existence.
Habitual unease. Guilt before appetite.
The long silence.

From my mother the iron junta of appearance.
The will to advance. Obsequious
Desire to please.

From the North Sea the weather of possibility.
Clear horizons. The imperative of poetry.
A salt asperity.

From the Oak Woods the press and curve
Of things. Incomparable whiteness of water lily.
The purple globe of figs.

From the Catholic Church the acid of doubt.
Magic of incantation. Anodyne of prayer.
The terrible seeking out.

The Silent One

Father, what have I made of you over the years?
The silent one. But, indeed, you were silent. Words

Dried in your mouth even before our conversation
Started and on Sundays at the back of the congregation

You would sing one false note, then try no more—
Red at the throat, flustered, self-deprecating to the core;

And before each shy feeling you were either violent,
Raging out with piston arms, or hugely silent:

Yours the inscrutable reticence I could not read . . .
So over the years you grew, a colossus in my head,

A statue of towering silence I had to break.
In smashing you I came to stutter, then to speak—

Hurling new words, shouting each quantum name:
A star out of guilt, a sun out of shame.

A Raw Planting

On visiting my parents' graves

Whatever the month it's much the same—the wind
Is bitter, stinging with salt, cut by showers
Of sleet or rain. At the iron gates the stunt pines stand
Monuments to endurance. And often I come with flowers

Wrenched from hedgerows, rank with seed,
Coarse with leaves. Today, though, it's bulbs bought
At West Runton, *Shakespearian Tulips*, starting to green.
Mother would have loved the name—with that hint

Of a superior strain. Father would have frowned:
What's the use, boy? Words will get you nowhere.
I force the bulbs into the hard memorial ground
And know for certain they'll not flower here—

Nor yet survive the winter blades of frost, blizzards
Of snow. But this raw planting must suffice.
In the distance the sea thunders in, gouging the cliffs,
Grinding the stone. My fingers hang like ice.

Flowering Gorse

Last night I dreamt of my father's grave.
It was on the cliff-top close to the abrading sea,
Now overgrown with nettles and vetch and gorse—

And I had no wish to cut down the scrub; I gave
Myself permission to let it all go, to let it be
What it was: prick of the spikes and coarse

Green of leaves, bent and warped by the cold—
And the small flowers—and the gold. And the gold.

Out of Touch

Father, forgive me; I have been out of touch too long;
No letters sent; no laconic rendezvous; no awkward words
Echoing in the underground of love's grievance: the wound
Of childhood, the changing nuances of your chafing silence.

Yet in a recent dream I saw you dressed in a pink suit
(So unlike you) and high on a dais you smiled and waved
As the high-tech train I was in moved smoothly out,
Hypnotically pulling into the future on insidious silver tracks.

Yes. It was you alright, waving and smiling. In the subway
Of dreams—crazy, surreal—was this your final farewell?
Your last gesture? But, father, I have one more thing to say:
I read less. On long journeys the book slips to my knees

As I watch the speechless green race by, the silent fields,
The dumb clouds. I no longer need the lexicon of hate
I hurled at you. Am ready now to hold your dying hands,
To mop your nightmare brow. Father, forgive me for arriving late.

It Returns

Further back in time, the war seems closer now,
Ricocheting in my ears, hardening like shrapnel
Buried in my anxious skin, blitzing hope. As a boy

It was otherwise. I would crawl through barbed wire
To the cliff's edge and stop vertiginous there, the sea salt
On my tongue—the gulls stretched overhead,

Gliding into the impossible. In ploughed fields nearby
The craters gouged by Nazi bombs buzzed and clicked
With insect life. A child's small Eden. Goldfinches blazed

From yellow gorse to yellow gorse. The air-raid shelter
Was our basement for hide and seek, a twilight maze
For idiotic play, spontaneous make-believe. The gas mask

Dangling from its wall a play-thing to tease the age.
That war seems nearer now, the natural light opaque.
Each day I hear Fascist strains rise from the street.

At night the eagle and the swastika are sprayed on local walls
Or cut with small metal coins deep into the glass.
And on corners I watch bald-headed boys waiting for the call

To smash the windows in, kick down the doors
And round the fuckers up, to see the metropolis on fire
And, grinning, from his armoured car, their brute Messiah.

The Flowering of Flint

Enter this gate between burial mounds; sheep bleat
Over chalk and grass, over the stunted ground
To disappear in a gap in the clouds. Enter this gate

And take the white track over the curving land.
Your shadow moves across the sepulchre
Of time. A hundred million immaculate years stand

Under your feet and the many implacable dead.
They breed fierce life: orchid, nettle and thistle
With its iron spikes and its purple tribal head.

What's gone comes back! What's buried resurrects!
Enter this gate and climb until you find the church;
Its sparse spire inspires, its crumbling wall protects.

Wait here. Pray here. Stay till you understand—
Until silver light glints through the broken tower
And the harsh flint flowers in your open hand.

Ecce Homo:
On Nietzsche's Madness

Against the Cold

6,000 feet above sea level and higher than all earthly things.

There are no flowers in the room. No ornaments;
No love letters on the cluttered desk or mantelpiece—
Only quack potions against migraine, sedatives

For sleep. Mesmerised by the march of metaphors
He writes and writes. Deep as the night they flow in,
Changing frontiers, disarranging, estranging. A fox stirs

In a steep track of white. A new moon slips between
Mountains and clouds. Is there some synchronicity here?
Some counterpoint? Or is it only chance? Unseen

Dramas coinciding at random? The man sits at the table;
Cramped fingers scribble his austere premonitions.
Being becoming. Silverdark. And incommensurable.

A virtual world rises between yes and no.
Outside it happens to grow dark. Begins to snow.

If You Should Meet Socrates

Only in the dance do I know how to tell the parable of the highest things.

If on the road you should meet Socrates—
And fail to kill him,

Then avoid his ironic eyes,
His enticing invitations,

Teasing aporias. Refuse to shake his hand,
Decline the olives and the wine.

And not one word in answer to his questions.
The smallest concept

Sparks the engine of his mind, that machine of refutation
No-one survives.

So, not one word of explanation,
Not one word of greeting.

Then, if he should pester you, be brave
And simply dance.

Let your body rise before him,
Every gesture conjunctive, assertion of your blood,

Your breath, your life,
Your death. An acrobatic child dancing on the grave,

A self-propelling wheel, a yes and (again) a yes.
Then, without a pause, pass on:

Artist, vessel of life, self-maker,
Seiltänzer.

Life as Dance

A will to mastery is required for thinking and it has to be learned the way dancing is learned.

Seiltänzer—that's it, that's your word, dancer or better still—
rope-walker,

one trained for thinking,
for stepping lightly.

Nothing superfluous.

The senses kindling the moment,
over the huddled crowds,
the past behind one.

Seiltänzer:
This is your word for living dangerously,
shuddering in mid-air,
standing still,
judging,

then stepping forward.

Each taut step on the humming rope
A triumph:

Ah life!

He lives well who lives lightly,
hoards nothing,
lets go the air he breathes—

to draw in more.

You call the art of being—
amor fati:
the love of fate—

on the trembling rope
each moment a dancing act:

concise,
consummate.

Under the Bell-Tower in Genoa: Summer 1877

Excess is the path to the übermench.

Such revelations fall uninvited. Descend in a moment. Meaning
So audacious there are no words. It pinpricks the skin,
Snuffs out the light of the intellect, up-ends the quotidian.
It was always waiting like this—bright as the glockenspiel

In a child's garden. For you it came one evening in Genoa
Listening to that carillon. How its music engulfed the square—
Filled the air, the tall bell-tower its epicentre. What did you hear?
Life singing its inexplicable aria? The shock of beauty there?

An overcoming? Something like that. And a sadness too.
You scribbled in your notebook: *Gravity through lightness;*
And then you half remembered a fragment from Plato:
Quite everything human is unworthy of high seriousness

But nevertheless—
                you recall the bells' urgent excess,
Needling our provisional humanity with its insatiable *yes.*

Seiltänzer

For dancing in any form cannot be divorced from a noble education,
being able to dance with the feet, with concepts, with words.

How eloquently you proclaimed the dance for life,
Life for the dance, life for those with agile feet,
A leap and a whirl wanting no further proof:
A candle lit, you said, self-sustaining, self-replete—

Yet always labile. Then did you know the Hindu Shiva
Dancing with his necklace of skulls, his hour-glass drum,
Bearing his burning wheel? One glance of his third eye
And a city was ash. And yet his dance, too, was one

Of affirmation. You would have relished that—a god
Worth saving. Indeed, when Alexander first saw Shiva
He thought he had been fashioned from divine
Dionysus—and that he too danced, the god of life:

Nataraja! But now I am perplexed by your twilight years:
Mit Nietzsche ist es aus! The dribbling incoherence.
No dance movement here. Nothing complete—
Smashing windows, bowing to doctors, heavy dragging feet.

At the Foot of the Alps

... there is a feeling of plenitude, the power which seeks to overflow, the happiness of high tension, the consciousness of a wealth which would fain give and bestow.

I hardly think of you at Naumberg,
Provincial northern town,

Black maw
Of respectability,

Which all but swallowed you
Returning in your madness,

The Anti-Christ
Clinging to your mother's skirts,

The immoralist
Bowing to Herr Docteur,

A pedantic,
Bewildered boy.

Nor do I think of your *Zarathustra*,
That unfree mimicry,

Impostor
Of hyperbole,

Your father
Lurching from the pulpit,

Christ on replay.
All those biblical cadences

And phrases
From your hated childhood days,

That too earnest sermon—
On play.

Rather, I think of you at the foot of the Alps
In your last chosen town.

Each thought plucked from the air
A revelation,

Each sensation
A courier with startling news.

A Shakespeare
Of unblotted aphorisms.

How to affirm the passing of things?
How to love transience?

All the comings and goings
In the street below:

The smell of bread,
Horses' rhythmic hooves,

Finch's cry,
Blizzard of contingencies,

The fact
That we must die.

Turin.
1888.

This I think of as your place
And time.

In the shadowed Renaissance square
The mind's

Crystalline fountain
Overflowing,

Pure bravura
Of being:

Dasein:
Being there.

In the Piazza: Turin, 3rd January 1889

Siamo contenti? Son dio, ha fatto questa caricatura: Are we happy?
I am God. I made this caricature.

It is early morning. I imagine a cold blue light,
Dry air, the winter sun
Almost warming the skin and you striding out

To embrace the day: the woman selling grapes,
Smell of bread, ground coffee,
The vendor's call. You feel a rising euphoria,

But today is not to be that kind of day—
For you have already heard
The crack of the whip, seen the cab-horse cower

And fall. And now you stare into its bloodshot eye,
A red orb of terror,
And almost at the same instant clasp its neck

To ward off further blows. Then start to cry.
When the landlord comes, guides you
To your room, the crowd parts to let you through -

And you go with the timidity of a child,
Almost too willing to please.
But that night you pace the floor, an abject beast,

And scream: *I am Dionysus . . . I am Alexander . . .*
Caesar-with-the-heart-of-Christ . . .
And hit for hours the black piano keys.

Prometheus and the Eagle

I was crucified last year
And go everywhere in my student overcoat.
I am God I made this caricature.
This Autumn I attended my funeral twice.

Questions, like waves, explode in the brain.
Anonymous the tide returns. At the beginning
Of our century the quarry's unchanged.

                                 Deaf
To the words wrought from our disenchantment,
Sublime discontent, unimaginable morning
Erupts again.

                    The ocean glints. Through a ring
Of callous blue the eagle hovers and drops;
The blood drips on the silent rocks.

The words darken the page. *I am a clown*
Of the new eternities. I promise a tragic age.

In the Psychiatric Clinic: Jena, 19th January 1889

It would have been a far more genuine act of friendship to take his life. I have now no other wish than that his life be taken from him.

Franz Overbeck to Peter Gast

All night without a break—incoherent chatter—
needs constant surveillance—

When I see on Rood
Jesu my lemen

—rips off his coat—lies on the ground—
sings—whimpers—shouts—

And beside Him standen
Mary and Johan

—breaks into chanting and screaming—
bursts of anger—

And his rig iswangen
And his side istungen

—Dionysus—Nietzsche Caesar—
The Crucified One—

Well ought I to wepen
And sins for to leten

If I of love can,
if I of love . . . if I of . . . if I . . . if—

Übermensch

*But I confess that the deepest objection to the Eternal Recurrence, my
real idea from the abyss, is always my mother and my sister.*

As his loving sister, she could have wheeled him
In his invalid's chair into any sunless lecture room
In Berlin or some much smaller provincial town—
Treblinka, Auschwitz, Belsen, Dachau—

And there asked him to preach on all his trenchant themes:
*The will to power, death of god, the birth of tragedy,
Übermensch.* And the students would have looked up
To see an imbecile, dribbling, head slumped, tongue

Stuttering incoherence: *Übermensch. Übermensch.*
And between long pauses they might have heard
Him pronounce: *I am God, I made this caricature.*
Or shout: *Maestro Pietro, sing me a new song.*

The world is transfigured, the stars shine out—
Or cry: *I had Caiaphas put in chains last night.
I am the clown of God . . . I am Dionysus Crucified.
Übermensch. Übermensch. Übermensch.*

And the students might have politely clapped.
But what his sister did was so much more unjust.
She took an axe to the green forest of his books
And hacked their flowering branches down,

To make a thousand numbered planks, to make
A thousand numbered trucks, to make a thousand
Numbered huts, to augur in the white apocalypse of ash.
Übermensch. Übermensch. Übermensch.

Requiescat in Pace

Nietzsche was buried at Röcken on August 25th 1900.

So now you are duly returned to where you were born:
The scrubbed village of Röcken. The church bell rings.
There's a silver cross screwed into your oak coffin.

The local choir dolefully render the traditional hymns.
Yet over the flat-lands there's a procession of clouds.
Ragged, inscrutable, sublime:
                              Dancers. Shamans. Clowns.

The Living Word

Ars Poetica

It will listen to the arias of whales.
It will wake to the dawn yelp of the gull.
It will affirm the blue canticle of the skylark, the black croak of
    the frog.

It will be schooled by the sibilance of water, be attuned to the
    hard consonance of rock.
It will gut dictionaries.
It will eat etymologies.
It will eavesdrop on the spontaneous ramblings of children.
It will tour fairgrounds with a microphone.

It will tremble before the glance of Beauty.

It will taste the white vinegar of death.

It will honour silence.

It will be a crucible open to stars and dust.
It will expound the laws of Quantum Mechanics and recite the
    Proverbs of Blake.

It will aspire to the levity of the butterfly crossing nuclear
    zones.

It will be born in blood, rise in estrangement, climax in breath.

It will remain in quest.

New Poems

Learning How Not to Live

What did I learn at school but the grammar of schism,
Tireless division of subject

And object, questions shut tight as an evangelist's fist,
The red catechism,

Clause analysis, problems with one correct answer
At the back of the book.

We put phrases in coffins and buried them neatly.
Where were the words

Which turned into kestrels on the wind's edge?
Where were the verbs

That flowered, dark cones of lilac at the window ledge
Or petalled the grass

Or scattered sharp hail against the hard glass?
The windows were shut.

We sat with our eyes down and learnt the sentence of stasis—
As though the querulous

Questions of life had to be always excised.
Each day—the chalk screech

Of our teachers' voices and the dry susurration of leaves
In the passage outside.

Witnessing

For John Pack

Tonight at the Church of a Hundred Doors, almost midnight,
And all lights extinguished, a chasm of darkness,

Then as the clock chimes twelve the huge door opens
And the bishop enters, a single candle in his staunch hand,

Proclaiming as he strolls: *Christos Anestis! Christos Anestis!*
And hearing his baritone voice and seeing the small light

We shout back at once: *Alithos Anestis! Alithos Anestis!*
And take our candles to be lit from the one flame,

As the flickering light threads and seams the dark . . .
Now, you must understand I am not a religious man;

Hold no dogmas, receive no sacraments, bow to no hierarchies—
Yet each year I find myself, leaning over this balcony,

Believing it all, a spectral child with spellbound eyes.
What do I feel exactly? How can I say? I hear the same chord

Striking my soul when I catch the first swallow zig-zagging
In from Africa. Or when I see blood red poppies blowing

Over the island's gravestones. Or when I throw open the window
Of our home to the Aegean breeze. It's why I left my home

And came to this ancient burial ground, seeking what I didn't know:
Christos Anestis! A myth for being here; the words for saying so.

Living with Aphrodite

The signs of the gods are perpetually scattered in places.
                                        Simplicius

I admire you, in May, most prodigious divinity who—
Long after alchemy—is still practical alchemist,
At the back of the house, quietly transmuting matter.

As we lie in each other's arms, climax and sleep
How in the yard outside the ivy spreads,
Spirals round the telephone wires, mounts plastic,

Greens the burglary alarms; and over rank drains
The indigenous honeysuckle climbs to flout
Her intoxicating scent, causal as life—trying it out

In an obscure corner. As Simplicius says; *the signs
of the gods are perpetually scattered*—here
and here and here. Utterly precise. Under punk walls

jagged with glass, in airless vaults, suburban cul-de-sacs,
urban spills and tips, the same surplus and sap.
Unflinching seed breaks through industrial tarmac.

In Praise of Chinese Soup

Because this morning you left at such a pace—
As you pulled on your winter coat
Not even time for a perfunctory kiss,

Shouting at the door a word I didn't get—
I forgot to tell you how much I love you.
I laboured all morning fretting the hours away

And lunched alone in a sunless kitchen finding
The Chinese soup you left. Absurd to say:
It was sublime. I had a second helping

And then, almost ashamed of my desire,
Kept going back to sip some more. I took a walk
Through the local woods. The wind was up;

A silver light flared through swaying branches.
Everywhere I looked rain-water glinted back;
Small birds flitted through bushes too quick

To catch—they were flying so fast a kind of chasm
Opened in my heart, a shaft so stark it had no end.
Rehearse death daily urge the Stoics. But today

I had no wish for the final tryst in the fable:
A last tick of the clock, the door opening
To no-one coming and no place else. I begged reprieve

And longed for the day to end: for you to be back
Taking off that winter coat, light warm on your face,
Two bowls of soup steaming on the table.

Eschatology

*Mayan civilization around 900 AD reached a pinnacle of achievement
to suddenly and inexplicably disappear leaving only ruins covered by
the rain forest.*

My art slumps where four roads intersect—
    a deadening, never-ending, swish
and thrum; nothing but traffic sliding north,

south, east, west. At mid-night
    the light's a clinical phosphorescence;
most days a drumming corridor of grey.

What and how to write? I think of civilizations:
    how suddenly some lurch, go off the screen
in the heart-leap of a second, leaving

hardly a glitch. I can see this Mayan girl
    strolling through the temple at Angkor,
a crimson flower pinned to her braided hair,

a lean youth playing a flute under an arch,
    scholars plotting the etymologies of words,
astronomers the science of the stars,

sculptors carving stone—and then wiped-out.
    Silence. The eschatology of tendril
and rhizome. Today I hazard nothing but roots

uplifting temples or motorways; unfinished epics
    with natural codas—a single kestrel on the breeze,
white blackthorn lacing the unfarmed fields.

The Way

Listen to the way words fall,
Making their own music,
How they expand, *prestissimo* some times,

Then fall away
Opening a silence
Like the cool that surrounds a flint

On the Downs or the quiet in a quadrangle
After the singing of plainchant,
Even that chill hiatus

Before an impending storm.
You have little choice but to respond,
For in the pause

Comes your next move. You are far from sure
Of your direction now,
Of where you are; you could flounder here

For hours, in the ever darkening light,
Looking for that shaft of yellow
Where a farm door

Opens—for one moment—to a kitchen:
Fire ablaze, the table laid
With plates, spoons, knives, a jug of flowers.

Finding Words

I have often heard it said that word and world
have fallen out of their ancestral marriage . . .

that the word now sublates through its own syntax,
whirls, dissolves, as it moves and flows . . .

like living by a coastal town when the sea mist blows in
erasing the red lighthouse, the ice cream cafe,

the small old-fashioned signposts . . . no essences,
language creating us . . .

and so we become . . . even as we speak . . . an open fiction,
a novel in the making,

a play of words . . .
and there are mornings when I wake early and think:

I can embrace this . . . more verbal wit please
and a wild clowning . . . *Enter Hamlet reading a book* . . .

but today my thinking is more carnal,
less speculative . . . I sense my sweating flesh,

an almost-terror burning on my skin . . . my mother's death . . .
how very real it was . . . no breaks

for jest . . . as the morphine clicked in
the scent of lavender rose from her bed . . .

sitting in the ward all night my book slipped from my hands . . .
nothing but moonlight, birds singing,

a trolley rattling down the corridor,
a scream ... I watched the laburnum shed its yellow radiance ...

such a long hot June ... how dumbly we falter in the press
and thick of things ... always to feel this ache

fretting the charred skin ....
I think of those who survive the ones they love ...

friend, father, sweet-heart ... yet scrawl their faith in life ...
or Blaise Pascal walking with anguish

under the haphazard stars ...
and sown in his crumpled coat his testament of fire.